The Thoughts That Creep In

Alicia Manthe

/ BookLeaf Publishing

India | USA | UK

Made with ❤ on the BookLeaf Publishing Platform
www.bookleafpub.in
www.bookleafpub.com

Dedication

To those that question their emotions in circles

Preface

Trying to push through loss can be difficult. Trying to get your footing to move forward with our too busy lives, can be even harder. I hope you can relate and understand you are not alone.

Acknowledgements

For all my loved ones that kept making sure I was holding my head high.

1. Realization

People love the *game* with me
The chase
The excitement
The idea
The butterflies
The first kiss
The first touches
The midnight conversations
The cosmic pull
The concept
Until they realize they have me

2. October

When it came it hit
Hard
Fast
Digging up memories and futures of lifetimes

That feeling in your chest
Pounding
Heavy
The weight too much to bear

Life still going on but things felt wrong
Slipping
Warped
Lost by yourself

The tears wouldn't stop
Infinite
Flowing
Puddles left in the wake

Sadness tightened its grip
Choking
Stillness

Not sure to let it take you or fight

The spirals swept in like clock work
Deeper
Desperate
The mind not settling on what to feel

31 days felt like years
Slow
Frozen
One month has taken it all

3. All that's Left

You set my soul on fire
Your absence leaves me in ashes
Scared of the wind

4. Fortune teller

A fortune teller once told me that I would lose my soul
mate.
She's the only one I've ever believed.
Randomly wondering if it was this person.
Or that one.
As time went on I felt silly for thinking what she said
was truth.
I see it clearly now.
It's you.

5. Lying to myself

I say I'm done
I get it
It's fine.
You're still sitting there
In the back of my mind.
I say I accept it
It's better this way
But I always find myself
Wishing you stayed.
I say it's over
The crying is gone
Eating is back
But the emptiness grows.
I say I won't long for you
I Let love go
But I hold onto memories
When our love was whole.
I say friends is enough
But it tears me apart
I know you felt it
How could I be not what you want.
All these lies
I tell myself

One day I might believe them

Maybe if I see you happy with someone else.

6. A Fraction

You made the world feel like it was safe to be me
To laugh loudly, To cry, To love in my way
You made my emotions feel like they shouldn't be
blocked out
To thrive fully, to be understood deeply
You made me feel at home
To be peaceful, to be warm, to be truly happy
All in just a turn of the earth
And I can only hope I offered you at least a fraction back

7. But...

I know, no amount of waiting
Will ever change your mind
Our circumstances are permanent
Nothing to change
But...
I can't help but see
Our future together
The sweetest moments
That haven't happen yet
How happy we could be
But...
It would be one sided
My happiness
And your loss

8. Close the door

I want to delete you
To pretend you are just gone
But I still see you
I still answer your call
I remove you from what I can
But you stay in my head
My heart breaks on repeat
Because we can't fully close the door

9. I already know

Will I ever see those pretty brown eyes
Look at me like I'm everything again
Will I feel your hand
Hold perfectly to mine
Will I ever see you laugh
The way we pushed against each other but held on tight
Will I ever feel the poetry
We created in the dark
Will I ever feel your squeeze
While we lay on your couch
Will I?
But I already know that answer

10. Homeless

Home never felt like home
But you did
And I fear I've lost that too

11. Leave the music off

It would be better
If I left the music off
Lyrics bring me to you
Rhythms bring me to the sweet moments
Melodies make me want to reach out to you
Harmonies bring the tears of what will never be
I should just leave the music off

12. Untitled

I should have believed you
Every time you said you were unsure

But I never questioned
If you loved me

13. We ended

We were on a high
In the bubble
We clicked
We loved
We talked deeply
We created safety
We laughed
And kissed
And as we peaked
We ended

14. Heart and brain

I don't want to continue loving you
My brains says stop
My heart says no
I don't want to tell you things
But your the first person
I open on my screen
I don't want to keep being reminded of you
But all things are some how attached
A smell
A mug
A book
A song
They lead back to you
I don't want to forget what we had
Heart heart says stop
And my brain says no

15. Over it

I'm over being strong
I'm over pretending I'm ok
I'm over being stuck in one spot
I'm over wondering if you think of me
I'm over my heart pounding when there's a chance you'll
be there
I'm over the tears
I'm over the tiredness
I'm over grieving what could have been
I'm over how things ended
I'm over how I tried to hold on
So why can't I be over you

16. The fantasy

I fantasize about waking up
And being happy
Feeling the sunshine on my skin
A warm breeze in my hair
Everyone laughing
Real smiles on my face
I'm terrified
That I'll never make that fantasy true

17. Not prepared

I have lived life
I have had wins and losses
Moments when my heart grew larger than I could
imagine
And times when I shrank to nothing
Scraped knees and kisses
Warm days and cold winter nights
But nothing could have prepared me for this
Like ripping half of my soul away
Letting a beautiful song get drowned out by the wind
Knowing it's better if I say nothing
Being silenced by wanting you to be happy
To say goodbye
So you can find your forever

18. Stuck in your tide

When will the gravity stop
And pull toward you loosen
When will it stop crushing me
And allow me to stand on my feet again
When will it stop feeling like your the moon
And I'm stuck in the high and low tides
When will I wake up
And be ok you're not with me

19. Jealous

I will always hope you are happy
And loved
And taken care of
And protected
And safe
And treasured
But I'll always be jealous that it's not by me

20. No one

No one will be you
The way you listened
And looked at me
The way you would hold me as I cried
The way you support my ideas
The way you inspired me
And gave me new perspective
No one will be you
The way you put a smile on my face
The way you made my heart beat
The way our hands fit together
The feeling I got when our lips collided
And our breath got heavy
No one will be you
They'll never compare

21. I hope you think of me

I hope you think of me
When you hear that song I would sing
I hope you think of me
When you eat food we use to get together
I hope you think of me
When a raven flies by
I hope you think of me
When you go dancing like we use to
I hope you think of me
When you smell coffee
I hope you think of me
When you go into the book store
I hope you think of me
When you look back and think of love

22. My last letter to you

I don't know what to do when you're heavy on my mind
and heart first thing in the morning.
Not knowing whether to stay and fight and show you
how I love you.
Or let you walk away like you said you wanted.
Half of me understands, I get it.
How could this ever be something you would want.
Really want.
I would be you settling.
The other half of me struggles because I can feel it.
And I know you do too.
Our connection,
Our love for eachother.
I'm pretending that I'm ok with you moving on.
I'm faking it to try to make it out of this hurt.
But I know deep down I want to run to you.
Back to the place that feels like home.
Where everything feels possible.
My chest is heavy,
And hearing you,
Seeing you.
Makes my heart want to escape back to you.
How I can see how happy we will always make
eachother,

But you cannot?

What did I miss?

My heart breaks because I want to be with you.

But it also breaks knowing you think you will be happier without me.

I want you to be happy.

I just wish it were me that brought you there.

My days are spent fighting the battle of what to do next,

How to forget,

How to hold on.

My nights are spent wondering how you are.

If you're ok.

if you ate.

If you're lonely.

If you miss me the same.

My mornings are dread of the leaving,

And my nights are filled with the impossible hope of us.

23. Help me

Can you just cut the ties
Tell me you don't want to be in my life or I yours
Tell me that you only respond out of being nice but you
don't care for anything I say
Tell me that you've been done with the idea of me and
that's all I ever was
Tell me it wasn't just fear you acted out on
Tell me I mean nothing to you

24. In the dark

I'm lost.

No one is going to come for me.

I don't know how to get out of this place.

I don't recognize myself here.

And I don't know if I care.

I don't know if I have anymore left to give,

To try,

To want.

I'm stuck.

All my moves feel wrong.

I feel dead inside.

I know I can't wait for someone to come.

I know I must push through.

But it's like I'm glued here.

The sun doesn't shine anymore.

And all the colors that use to be so vibrant and beautiful

Are dulled.

Muted.

Disappearing.

How do I bring them back.

How can I even possibly hope for it.

In the dark.

All alone.

Empty.

25. Our own hearts

What a silly me
To forget reality and allow myself to daydream.
To want more than I know life will give me.
Oh,
The way we can break our own hearts

26. Your love

I don't think the timing will ever be right,
But you were definitely the right one.

I wanted your love,
Without convincing you of it.

27. The unknown

All the life she thought was left her eyes in one moment.
It was mirage, just something that looked to be an oasis
from far away.
Pieces fell into place showing her the remnants of what
could have been
And what never really was.
While stuck in the mud she had to do something,
Panic setting in.
Not being able to see in front of her,
She had to take the next step forward.
Working up the courage to go into the unknown.
At this point there should be nothing to fear.
If she steps to failure what's one more.

With no one left to help pick up the pieces,
She has to find a way to get them all back,
And glue them back together.
In order to protect the little hearts,
She has to pretend hers is still whole.
Autopilot has taken over.
And though she truly cares she can't care at all.

As she moves through this maze to escape the pain,
She can't find the path.

Shes getting turned around,
Falling in tracts and finding herself back in the same
place.
Every move she makes leads to her back to the same
place.
No matter how different her choice.
It's always the same ending,
The darkness makes sure of it.

28. I'm sorry

Life can be a cruel joke
One minute it shows you what it could be
All the light, laughter, emotions, security
Then you are saying I'm in love with you to a person
that responds with I'm sorry...